The Ave Guide to the
Scriptural Rosary

"What an excellent book, filled with beautiful religious art! This is a must-have book for all who pray the Rosary: beginners, intermediates, and advanced. It is chock-full of scriptural quotations that will take you deeper into the wonder of the Greatest Story Ever Told: the life of Jesus, Mary, and Joseph on earth."

Fr. Francis Joseph "Fr. Rocky" Hoffman
Chairman and CEO of Relevant Radio
and host of *The Family Rosary Across America*

"*The Ave Guide to the Scriptural Rosary* will strengthen the special bond that ties together so many of our Holy Cross apostolates in the United States and throughout the world. From our very foundation, the Congregation has held close Our Lady of Sorrows as our patroness and the Rosary as our special prayer, and our apostolates have been grounded in devotion to her. Our perennial hope and promise is that praying the Rosary will bring families, our Church, and all of society together in a strengthened bond of love in these complex times."

Fr. William Lies
Provincial Superior
Congregation of Holy Cross, United States Province
of Priests and Brothers

"This book offers an excellent catechesis on the Rosary: its origins, the graces that come from praying it, and what the Church teaches about it. This guide implicitly answers questions such as Where do I direct my prayer?, Is the focus on Mary or on Jesus Christ?, and What should I be meditating on while I pray the prayers? This book is for those who have never prayed the Rosary and need to learn the basics, as well as for those who have offered these prayers for years and years. As one who loves the Rosary—and who prayed it nightly with my siblings and parents while we lived at home—I highly recommend this book and this important and grace-filled devotion!"

Bishop William A. Wack
Diocese of Pensacola–Tallahassee

"Anyone who has had trouble focusing on the mysteries of the Rosary will find a treasure in this little book. It skillfully blends scripture with contemplative prayer, focusing the mind and engaging the heart in a deep encounter with our Lord and his mother. As you pray the words of scripture, you will enter the very scenes of Jesus's life as you learn to hear and recognize the voice of God."

Sarah Christmyer
Author of *Becoming Women of the Word*

"The Rosary is such a beautiful prayer. Oftentimes it can be hard to slow down and enjoy the richness of the prayers and the mysteries. *The Ave Guide to the Scriptural Rosary* has completely changed how I pray the Rosary. I am no longer simply reciting prayers—I am praying in a slow, peaceful manner and growing through meaningful reflection on the mysteries of Jesus and Mary."

Susan Wallace
Director of External Relations
Holy Cross Family Ministries

The Ave Guide to the
Scriptural
Rosary

AVE MARIA PRESS AVE Notre Dame, Indiana

Nihil Obstat: Reverend Monsignor Michael Heintz, PhD
            Censor Librorum

Imprimatur: Most Reverend Kevin C. Rhoades
            Bishop of Fort Wayne–South Bend

Given at: Fort Wayne, Indiana, on September 13, 2022

Writer
Michael Amodei

© 2023 by Ave Maria Press, Inc.

Founded in 1865, Ave Maria Press is a ministry of the United States Province of Holy Cross.

www.avemariapress.com

Paperback: ISBN-13 978-1-64680-190-9

E-book: ISBN-13 978-1-64680-191-6

Cover design by Christopher D. Tobin.

Text design by Kristen Hornyak Bonelli.

Printed and bound in the United States of America.

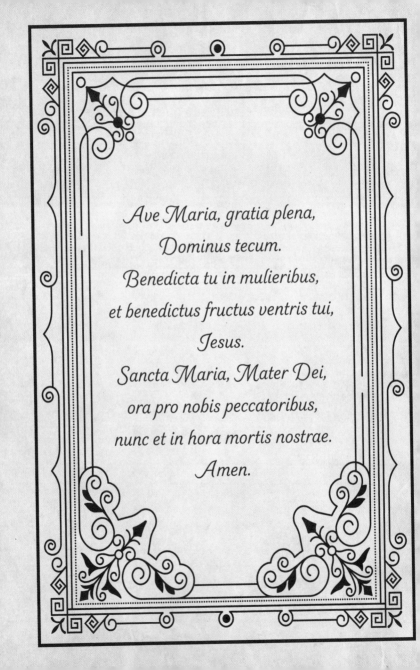

Ave Maria, gratia plena,
Dominus tecum.
Benedicta tu in mulieribus,
et benedictus fructus ventris tui,
Jesus.
Sancta Maria, Mater Dei,
ora pro nobis peccatoribus,
nunc et in hora mortis nostrae.
Amen.

Contents

Preface

More than 155 years since our founding, Ave Maria Press, an apostolate of the Congregation of Holy Cross, with our home on the campus of the University of Notre Dame, brings you this book of scriptural reflections on the culmination of God's redemption in the Divine Person of his Son, Jesus Christ, through the intimate cooperation of his Mother, the Blessed Virgin Mary. The prayerful reflections are organized around the four mysteries of the Holy Rosary.

A perennial part of the mission of Ave Maria Press is to honor Mary, for whom we are named. Fr. Edward Sorin, CSC, our founder, believed that the company's original weekly magazine, *The Ave Maria*, and all of its subsequent publications would be "the source of most abundant blessings, one of the best things ever done in the Congregation, and ultimately a glorious work for our Blessed Mother."

The Holy Rosary—Mary's prayer—is interwoven with our company's history and tradition. We have published dozens of books on the practice and graces of the Rosary over the years. The Congregation of Holy Cross is also the proud home of the Venerable Fr. Patrick Peyton, known as "the Rosary priest" who led millions to pray the Rosary in the mid-twentieth century. Fr. Peyton studied at Holy Cross Minor Seminary, just across the road from our current location in between St. Joseph's and St. Mary's Lakes at Notre Dame.

We offer you this new scriptural Rosary companion to continue the commitment of our Holy Cross founders and partners to bring honor to Notre Dame du Lac, Our Lady of the Lakes. May it help you to grow in love for her and her Son, Our Savior.

Introduction

The various eras of the Church are wrought with different influences, practices, and charisms. Yet, the Holy Rosary, a devotion to Mary, the Blessed Mother of God, not only persists but is also rediscovered and reborn anew in each generation.

Think about the technological, cultural, and spiritual changes over the past century. There has been the invention of the combustion engine, two world wars, a space age, yearly advances in communication media, and much more. In the Church, there was an ecumenical council and its ramifications. Yet all of the popes since the turn of the twentieth century have commended the Rosary and brought to the fore the importance of this devotion not only for the Church herself but also for the world as a whole. Consider these sentiments on the Holy Rosary:

Pope Leo XIII
(1878–1903)

"The Rosary is the most excellent form of prayer. It is the remedy for all our evils, the root of all blessings. There is no more excellent way of praying."

Pope St. Pius X
(1903–1914)

"The Rosary is the most beautiful and the richest of all prayers to Mediatrix of all grace; it is the prayer that touches most the heart of the Mother of God."

Pope Benedict XV
(1914–1922)

"The Most Holy Rosary is a prayer that 'is most adapted to fostering widely piety and every virtue.'" (*Fausto Appetente Die*, 11)

Pope Pius XI
(1922–1939)

"Kings and princes, however burdened with most urgent occupations and affairs, made it their duty to recite the Rosary." (*Ingravescentibus Malis*, 15)

Pope Pius XII
(1939–1958)

"Truly, from the frequent meditation on the Mysteries, the soul little by little and imperceptibly draws and absorbs the virtues they contain, and is wondrously enkindled with a longing for things immortal, and becomes strongly and easily to follow the path which Christ himself and his Mother have followed." (*Ingruentium Malorum*, 9)

Pope St. John XXIII
(1958–1963)

"These pleasant memories of our younger days have not faded or vanished as the years of our life have passed. On the contrary, we want to declare in complete frankness and simplicity that the years have made Mary's Rosary all the dearer to us. We never fail to recite it each day in its entirety." (*Grata Recordatio*, 3)

Pope St. Paul VI
(1963–1978)

"We like to think, and sincerely hope, that when the family gathering becomes a time of prayer, the Rosary is a frequent and favored manner of praying." (*Marialis Cultus*, 54)

Blessed Pope John Paul I
(1978)

"The Rosary expresses the faith without false complications, without evasion, without lots of words; it helps us to abandon ourselves to God's will and to learn the generous acceptance of suffering."

Pope St. John Paul II
(1978–2005)

"The Rosary mystically transports us to Mary's side as she is busy watching over the human growth of Christ in the home of Nazareth. This enables her to train us and to mold us with the same care, until Christ is 'fully formed' in us." (*Rosarium Virginis Mariae*, 15)

Pope Benedict XVI
(2005–2013)

"The Rosary is a school of contemplation and silence. At first glance, it could seem a prayer that accumulates words, therefore difficult to reconcile with the silence that is rightly recommended for meditation and contemplation. In fact, this cadent repetition of the Hail Mary does not disturb inner silence but indeed both demands and nourishes it." (*Meditation at the Pontifical Shrine of Pompeii*, 3)

Pope Francis
(2013–present)

"In the prayer of the Rosary we turn to the Virgin Mary so that she may bring us ever closer to her Son Jesus, so as to know him and to love him more and more. This simple prayer, in fact, helps us to contemplate all that God in his love has done for us and for our salvation, and allows us to understand that our life is united to that of Christ." (*Video Message to the Bishop of Gozo*, 3)

From the words of the popes, we learn that the Rosary is not only devotional but also meditative and contemplative. It is a family prayer. Praying the Rosary brings the benefits of God's grace. Although it is a Marian prayer, the Rosary is, in the words of St. John Paul II, a "Christocentric prayer." John Paul II added that "with the Rosary, the Christian people sits at the school of Mary and is led to contemplate the beauty on the face of Christ and to experience the depths of his love" (*Rosarium Virginis Mariae*, 1).

What Is the Rosary?

The Rosary is also one of the most valued and practiced prayers in the Catholic Church. It is the greatest and most popular devotion to Mary, but above all, it is a meditation on the life of Christ. As our fingers move along the beads, our lips recite words of praise to Mary (the Hail Mary) while our minds and hearts remain fixed on scenes from Jesus's life. Our entire being is engaged in prayer. So, it's not surprising to learn that praying the Rosary has been encouraged and practiced by virtually every pope since its inception; even Mary herself has championed the Rosary in several of her apparitions.

A traditional story of the Rosary's origins is connected with a vision St. Dominic had of the Virgin Mary in 1214 in which she presented him with the Rosary, both the beads and the prayers that were to be prayed. However, Christians had been praying a version of the Hail Mary prayer for centuries before. Pope Gregory the Great, who was pope from 590 to 604, called for an early formation of the Hail Mary to be prayed on the fourth Sunday of Advent. People began to say a series of Hail Marys, often keeping track of the number by counting with beads. Praying with beads was and still is practiced by other faiths and cultures—for example, Hindus and Buddhists.

The form of the Rosary we know today evolved between the twelfth and fifteenth centuries. Eventually, 150 Hail Marys were linked with verses of the 150 psalms and with other passages that reminded people of the lives of Jesus and Mary. The Hail Marys were arranged in three sets of mysteries from the lives of Jesus and his mother known as the Joyful Mysteries, the Sorrowful Mysteries, and the Glorious Mysteries. Each set is made up of five decades of Hail Marys, a total of fifty in each set. Because the 150 Hail Marys corresponded to the 150 psalms, the Rosary became known as Mary's Psalter.

In October 2002, to begin a Year of the Rosary (October is the month of the Rosary), Pope St. John Paul II published an apostolic letter, *Rosarium Virginis Mariae* (*On the Most Holy Rosary*), to mark the beginning of the twenty-fifth year of his pontificate. In this letter, the pope added a new set of mysteries to the Rosary— the Luminous Mysteries or Mysteries of Light. Today, Catholics pray a total of two hundred Hail Marys while meditating on all of the mysteries of the Rosary.

How to Pray the Rosary

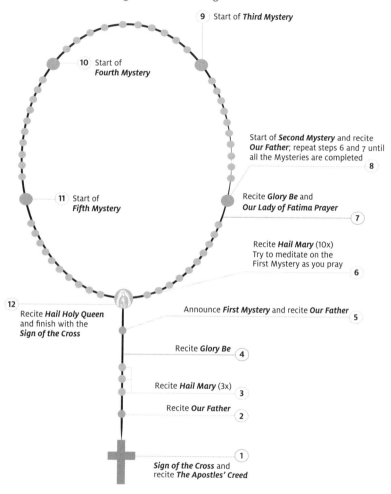

9 Start of *Third Mystery*

10 Start of *Fourth Mystery*

Start of *Second Mystery* and recite *Our Father*; repeat steps 6 and 7 until all the Mysteries are completed **8**

11 Start of *Fifth Mystery*

Recite *Glory Be* and *Our Lady of Fatima Prayer* **7**

Recite *Hail Mary* (10x) Try to meditate on the First Mystery as you pray **6**

12 Recite *Hail Holy Queen* and finish with the *Sign of the Cross*

Announce *First Mystery* and recite *Our Father* **5**

Recite *Glory Be* **4**

Recite *Hail Mary* (3x) **3**

Recite *Our Father* **2**

1 *Sign of the Cross* and recite *The Apostles' Creed*

To pray the Rosary, we recite a series of prayers while reflecting on the events from Christ's Incarnation and hidden years in Jerusalem (Joyful Mysteries), his proclamation of God's kingdom (Luminous Mysteries), his Passion and Death (Sorrowful Mysteries), and his Resurrection and Ascension (Glorious Mysteries). The final two sets of Glorious Mysteries are meditations on Mary's assumption into heaven and her coronation as Queen of heaven and earth.

The recitation of prayers is not the focus of praying the Rosary. Rather, their repetitive nature serves as a type of mantra in a regular rhythm that keeps us centered on the particular mystery on which we are meditating. Praying the Rosary is divided into three parts: the opening, the body, and the conclusion. Directions for praying the Rosary follow.

The Opening

Begin on the crucifix, and pray the Apostles' Creed.

Apostles' Creed

> I believe in God,
> the Father almighty,
> Creator of heaven and earth,

and in Jesus Christ, his only Son, Our
    Lord,
who was conceived by the Holy Spirit,
born of the Virgin Mary,
suffered under Pontius Pilate,
was crucified, died, and was buried;
he descended into hell;
on the third day he rose again from the
    dead;
he ascended into heaven,
and is seated at the right hand of God
    the Father almighty;
from there he will come to judge the
    living and the dead.
I believe in the Holy Spirit,
the holy catholic Church,
the communion of saints,
the forgiveness of sins,
the resurrection of the body,
and life everlasting.
Amen.

On the first large bead, pray the Our Father.

Our Father, who art in heaven,
hallowed be thy name;
thy kingdom come,
thy will be done
on earth as it is in heaven.
Give us this day our daily bread,
and forgive us our trespasses,
as we forgive those who trespass against
us;
and lead us not into temptation,
but deliver us from evil.
Amen.

On the next three small beads, pray the Hail Mary. Meditate on the theological virtues of faith, hope, and charity on these beads.

Faith is a gift from God that can only exist with God's preceding grace. It is an act of a person's intellect, an assenting to the divine truth by command of the will that has been moved by grace. Though only possible by grace and the interior helps of the Holy Spirit, faith is a truly human action.

Hope enables us to firmly trust in God's gift of salvation and to be sure that he will bless us with the necessary gifts to attain it.

Charity is the greatest of the three theological virtues by which we love God above all else for his own sake, and our neighbor as ourselves out of love for God.

Hail Mary

> Hail, Mary, full of grace,
> the Lord is with thee.
> Blessed art thou among women,
> and blessed is the fruit of thy womb,
>   Jesus.
> Holy Mary, Mother of God,
> pray for us sinners,
> now and at the hour of our death.
> Amen.

On the next large bead, pray the Glory Be and the Fatima Prayer.

Glory Be

> Glory be to the Father,
> and to the Son,

and to the Holy Spirit,
as it was in the beginning,
is now,
and ever shall be,
world without end.
Amen.

Fatima Prayer

O My Jesus,
forgive us our sins,
save us from the fires of hell;
lead all souls to heaven,
especially those most in need
of thy mercy.
Amen.

The Body

On the large bead, announce the mystery to be prayed
and pray one Our Father.

On each of the ten small beads, pray one Hail
Mary while meditating on the mystery.

Pray one Glory Be and one Fatima Prayer at the end of the decade. (There is no bead for the Glory Be or the Fatima Prayer.)

The Conclusion

Pray the Salve Regina at the end of five decades of the Rosary.

Salve Regina (Hail, Holy Queen)

Hail, Holy Queen, Mother of Mercy,
our life, our sweetness, and our hope.
To thee do we cry,
poor banished children of Eve.
To thee do we send up our sighs,
mourning and weeping in this valley
    of tears.
Turn then, most gracious advocate,
thine eyes of mercy toward us,
and after this our exile,
show unto us the blessed fruit of thy
    womb, Jesus.
O clement, O loving,
O sweet Virgin Mary.
V. Pray for us, O holy Mother of God,

R. That we may be made worthy of
the promises of Christ.

When Pope St. John Paul II introduced a fourth set
of mysteries, the Luminous Mysteries, he also offered
suggestions for particular days on which to pray the
four sets: Joyful Mysteries on Mondays and Satur-
days, Luminous Mysteries on Thursdays, Sorrowful
Mysteries on Tuesdays and Fridays, and the Glorious
Mysteries on Wednesdays and Sundays.

Spiritual Graces of the Rosary

One of Mary's titles is "Mother of Divine Grace."
She is the Mother of Divine Grace because she is the
Mother of God, who is the Author of all grace. St.
Maximillian Kolbe, who had great devotion to Mary
and to praying the Rosary, understood Mary as the
Mediatrix ("female mediator") of all the graces of
the Holy Spirit. He described Mary as the "Created
Immaculate Conception" and the Holy Spirit as the
"Uncreated Immaculate Conception." Hence, Mary
herself is a dispenser of grace. The greeting of the
angel Gabriel teaches us that Mary is "favored" or
"full of grace" (see Lk 1:28).

The Fifteen Promises of Mary to Those Who Pray the Rosary

In the fifteenth century, a Dominican preacher, Bl. Alanus de Rupe, was concerned with the Albigensian heresy that falsely taught that all matter is evil, the spirit is good, and the two essentially oppose each other. Having little success with dissuading this heresy by his preaching, de Rupe increased his devotion to praying the Rosary. During this time, he had a vision of Mary appearing to St. Dominic, during which she gave Dominic a rosary to combat Albigensianism along with fifteen promises to those who pray the Rosary. The promises, though classified as a private revelation (which a Catholic is free to believe or not), remain a popular tradition in the Church. Mary's words are as follows:

1. Whoever shall faithfully serve me by the recitation of the Rosary shall receive singular graces.

2. I promise my special protection and the greatest graces to all those who shall recite the Rosary.

3. The Rosary shall be a powerful armor against hell; it will destroy vice, decrease sin, and defeat heresies.

4. It will cause virtue and good works to flourish; it will obtain for souls the abundant mercy of God; it will withdraw the hearts of people from the love of the world and its vanities, and will lift them up to the desire of eternal things. Oh, that souls would sanctify themselves by this means.

5. The soul which recommends itself to me by the recitation of the Rosary shall not perish.

6. Whoever shall recite the Rosary devoutly, applying themselves to the considerations of the sacred mysteries, shall never be conquered by misfortune. God will not chastise them in his justice; they shall not perish by an unprovided death; if they be just, they shall remain in the grace of God and become worthy of eternal life.

7. Whoever shall have a true devotion for the Rosary shall not die without the sacraments of the Church.

8. Those who are faithful to the recitation of the Rosary shall have, during their life and at their death, the light of God and the plentitude of his graces; at the moment of death they shall participate in the merits of the saints in paradise.

9. I shall deliver from purgatory those who have been devoted to the Rosary.

10. The faithful children of the Rosary shall merit a high degree of glory in heaven.

11. You shall obtain all you ask of me by the recitation of the Rosary.

12. All those who propagate the holy Rosary shall be aided by me in their necessities.

13. I have obtained from my Divine Son that all the advocates of the Rosary shall have for intercessors the entire celestial court during their life and at the hour of death.

14. All who recite the Rosary are my sons and daughters, and brothers and sisters of my only Son, Jesus Christ.

15. Devotion to my Rosary is a great sign of predestination.

How to Use a Scriptural Rosary

Pope St. Paul VI described the Rosary as the "compendium of the entire Gospel" and added that the "litany-like succession of Hail Mary's becomes an unceasing praise of Christ" (*Marialis Cultus*, 42, 46). *The Ave Guide to the Scriptural Rosary* provides scripture references for each of the mysteries of the Rosary.

Praying a scriptural Rosary is akin to the ancient practice of lectio divina ("sacred reading"), a component of the Liturgy of the Hours. Through the prayerful reading of God's Word, a person can encounter God and be led by the Holy Spirit to a deeper union with him. The method of this prayer involves taking a short scripture passage, reading it slowly and attentively, and letting your imagination, emotions, memory, desires, and thoughts engage the written text.

In a scriptural Rosary, you read a verse before saying a Hail Mary (*lectio*), meditate on its connection to the overall mystery (*meditatio*), and further contemplate (*contemplatio*) its place in the entire life of Christ and in God's plan for our salvation. After some time praying with these scripture verses, you will have them memorized and they will become a valuable aid in your meditative prayer life.

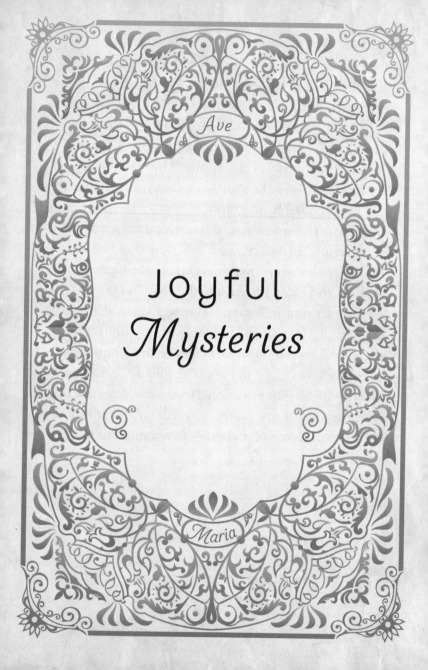

Ave

Joyful
Mysteries

Maria

For we were the purpose of his
embodiment, and for our salvation
he so loved human beings as to come
to be and appear in a human body.

—St. Athanasius of Alexandria

First
Joyful Mystery
The Annunciation

Our Father

> The angel Gabriel was sent from God . . . to a virgin betrothed to a man named Joseph, . . . and the virgin's name was Mary. (Lk 1:26–27)

Hail Mary

> And coming to her, he said, "Hail, favored one! The Lord is with you." (Lk 1:28)

Hail Mary

> She was greatly troubled at what was said and pondered what sort of greeting this might be. (Lk 1:29)

Hail Mary

Then the angel said to her, "Do not be afraid, Mary, for you have found favor with God." (Lk 1:30)

Hail Mary

"Behold, you will conceive in your womb and bear a son, and you shall name him Jesus." (Lk 1:31)

Hail Mary

"He will be great and will be called Son of the Most High, . . . and of his kingdom there will be no end." (Lk 1:32–33)

Hail Mary

Mary said to the angel, "How can this be, since I have no relations with a man?" (Lk 1:34)

Hail Mary

"The holy Spirit will come upon you, and the power of the Most High will overshadow you. Therefore the child to be born will be holy, the Son of God." (Lk 1:35)

Hail Mary

"And behold, Elizabeth, your relative, has also conceived a son in her old age . . . for nothing will be impossible for God." (Lk 1:36–37)

Hail Mary

Mary said, "Behold, I am the handmaid of the Lord. May it be done to me according to your word." (Lk 1:38)

Hail Mary

Glory Be

Fatima Prayer

Second

Joyful Mystery

The Visitation

Our Father

> Mary set out and traveled to the hill country in haste to a town of Judah, where she entered the house of Zechariah and greeted Elizabeth. (Lk 1:39–40)

Hail Mary

> When Elizabeth heard Mary's greeting, the infant leaped in her womb. (Lk 1:41)

Hail Mary

> Elizabeth, filled with the holy Spirit, cried out in a loud voice and said, "Most blessed are you among women, and blessed is the fruit of your womb." (Lk 1:41–42)

Hail Mary

"And how does this happen to me, that the mother of my Lord should come to me? For at the moment the sound of your greeting reached my ears, the infant in my womb leaped for joy." (Lk 43–44)

Hail Mary

And Mary said: "My soul proclaims the greatness of the Lord; my spirit rejoices in God my savior. For he has looked upon his handmaid's lowliness." (Lk 46–48)

Hail Mary

"Behold, from now on will all ages call me blessed. The Mighty One has done great things for me, and holy is his name" (Lk 1:48–49)

Hail Mary

"His mercy is from age to age to those who fear him. He has shown might with his arm, dispersed the arrogant of mind and heart." (Lk 1:50–51)

Hail Mary

"He has thrown down the rulers from their thrones but lifted up the lowly." (Lk 1:52)

Hail Mary

"The hungry he has filled with good things; the rich he has sent away empty." (Lk 1:53)

Hail Mary

"He has helped Israel his servant, remembering his mercy, according to his promise to our fathers, to Abraham and to his descendants forever." (Lk 1:55)

Hail Mary

Glory Be

Fatima Prayer

Second: The Visitation

Third

Joyful Mystery

The Nativity

Our Father

> Joseph too went . . . to the city of David
> that is called Bethlehem, . . . to be enrolled
> with Mary, his betrothed, who was with
> child. While they were there, the time
> came for her to have her child. (Lk 2:4–6)

Hail Mary

> She gave birth to her firstborn son. She
> wrapped him in swaddling clothes. (Lk 2:7)

Hail Mary

> And [she] laid him in a manger, because
> there was no room for them in the inn.
> (Lk 2:7)

Hail Mary

The Word became flesh and made his dwelling among us. (Jn 1:14)

Hail Mary

Now there were shepherds in that region living in the fields and keeping the night watch over the flock. The angel of the Lord appeared to them and the glory of the Lord shone around them, and they were struck with great fear. (Lk 2:8–9)

Hail Mary

The angel said to them, "Do not be afraid; for behold, I proclaim to you good news of great joy that will be for all people." (Lk 2:10)

Hail Mary

"For today in the city of David a savior has been born for you who is Messiah and Lord." (Lk 2:11)

Hail Mary

"And this will be a sign for you: you will find an infant wrapped in swaddling clothes and lying in a manger." (Lk 2:12)

Hail Mary

And suddenly there was a multitude of the
heavenly host with the angel, praising God
and saying: "Glory to God in the highest
and on earth peace to those on whom his
favor rests." (Lk 2:13–14)

Hail Mary

So [the shepherds] went in haste and
found Mary and Joseph, and the infant
lying in the manger. When they saw this,
they made known the message that had
been told them about this child. And Mary
kept all these things, reflecting on them in
her heart. (Lk 2:16–17, 19)

Hail Mary

Glory Be

Fatima Prayer

Fourth

Joyful Mystery

The Presentation

Our Father

> When the days were completed for their purification according to the law of Moses, they took [Jesus] up to Jerusalem to present him to the Lord. (Lk 2:22)

Hail Mary

> Now there was a man in Jerusalem whose name was Simeon. This man was righteous and devout, awaiting the consolation of Israel, and the holy Spirit was upon him. (Lk 2:25)

Hail Mary

> It had been revealed to him by the holy Spirit that he should not see death before

he had seen the Messiah of the Lord. (Lk 2:26)

Hail Mary

When the parents brought in the child Jesus to perform the custom of the law in regard to him, [Simeon] took him into his arms and blessed God. (Lk 2:27–28)

Hail Mary

"Now, Master, you may let your servant go in peace, according to your word." (Lk 2:29)

Hail Mary

"For my eyes have seen your salvation, which you have prepared in sight of all the peoples." (Lk 2:30–31)

Hail Mary

"A light for revelation to the Gentiles, and glory for your people Israel." (Lk 2:32)

Hail Mary

And Simeon blessed them and said to Mary his mother, "Behold, this child is destined for the fall and rise of many in Israel, and to be a sign that will be contradicted." (Lk 2:34)

Hail Mary

"And you yourself a sword will pierce." (Lk 2:35)

Hail Mary

When they had fulfilled all the prescriptions of the law of the Lord, they returned to Galilee, to their own town of Nazareth. The child grew and became strong, filled with wisdom; and the favor of God was upon him. (Lk 2:39–40)

Hail Mary

Glory Be

Fatima Prayer

Fourth: The Presentation

Fifth

Joyful Mystery

The Finding
in the Temple

Our Father

> Each year his parents went to Jerusalem
> for the feast of Passover, and when [Jesus]
> was twelve years old, they went up accord-
> ing to festival custom. (Lk 2:41–42)

Hail Mary

> After they had completed its days, as they
> were returning, the boy Jesus remained
> behind in Jerusalem, but his parents did
> not know it. (Lk 2:43)

Hail Mary

> Thinking that he was in the caravan, they
> journeyed for a day and looked for him
> among their relatives and acquaintances,

but not finding him, they returned to Jerusalem to look for him. (Lk 2:44–45)

Hail Mary

After three days they found him in the temple, sitting in the midst of the teachers, listening to them and asking them questions. (Lk 2:46)

Hail Mary

And all who heard him were astounded at his understanding and his answers. (Lk 2:47)

Hail Mary

When his parents saw him, they were astonished, and his mother said to him, "Son, why have you done this to us? Your father and I have been looking for you with great anxiety." (Lk 2:48)

Hail Mary

And he said to them, "Why were you looking for me? Did you not know that I must be in my Father's house?" (Lk 2:49)

Hail Mary

> But they did not understand what he said to them. (Lk 2:50)

Hail Mary

> He went down with them and came to Nazareth, and was obedient to them; and his mother kept all these things in her heart. (Lk 2:51)

Hail Mary

> And Jesus advanced [in] wisdom and age and favor before God and man. (Lk 2:52; brackets in the original)

Hail Mary

Glory Be

Fatima Prayer

Salve Regina

Luminous
Mysteries

Ave Maria

To carry out the will of the Father,
Christ inaugurated the kingdom of
heaven on earth and revealed to us
the mystery of that kingdom. By his
obedience he brought about redemption. The Church, or, in other words,
the kingdom of Christ now present
in mystery, grows visibly through the
power of God in the world.

—*Lumen Gentium*, 2

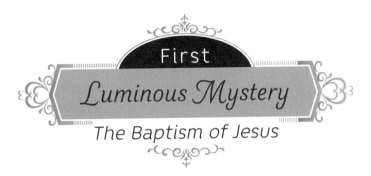

First
Luminous Mystery
The Baptism of Jesus

Our Father

> In those days John the Baptist appeared preaching in the desert of Judea and saying, "Repent, for the kingdom of heaven is at hand!" (Mt 3:1)

Hail Mary

> Now the people were filled with expectation, and all were asking in their hearts whether John might be the Messiah. (Lk 3:15)

Hail Mary

> John answered them all, saying, "I am baptizing you with water, but one mightier than I is coming. I am not worthy to loosen the thongs of his sandals." (Lk 3:16)

Hail Mary

> "He will baptize you with the holy Spirit and fire." (Lk 3:16)

Hail Mary

> The next day he saw Jesus coming toward him and said, "Behold, the Lamb of God, who takes away the sin of the world." (Jn 1:29)

Hail Mary

> Then Jesus came from Galilee to John at the Jordan to be baptized by him. John tried to prevent him, saying, "I need to be baptized by you, and yet you are coming to me?" (Mt 3:13–14)

Hail Mary

> Jesus said to him in reply, "Allow it now, for thus it is fitting for us to fulfill all righteousness." (Mt 3:15)

Hail Mary

> After Jesus was baptized, he came up from the water and behold, the heavens were

opened [for him], and he saw the Spirit of God descending like a dove [and] coming upon him. (Mt 3:16; brackets in the original)

Hail Mary

John testified, "I did not know him, but the one who sent me to baptize me with water told me, 'On whomever you see the Spirit come down and remain, he is the one who will baptize with the holy Spirit.'" (Jn 1:33)

Hail Mary

And a voice came from the heavens, saying, "This is my beloved Son, with whom I am well pleased." (Mt 3:17)

Hail Mary

Glory Be

Fatima Prayer

Second
Luminous Mystery

The Wedding Feast
at Cana

Our Father

> There was a wedding in Cana in Galilee, and the mother of Jesus was there. Jesus and his disciples were also invited to the wedding. (Jn 2:1–2)

Hail Mary

> When the wine ran short, the mother of Jesus said to him, "They have no wine." (Jn 2:3)

Hail Mary

> [And] Jesus said to her, "Woman, how does this concern affect me? My hour has not yet come." (Jn 2:4; brackets in the original)

His mother said to the servers, "Do whatever he tells you." (Jn 2:5)

Hail Mary

Now there were six stone water jars there for Jewish ceremonial washings, each holding twenty to thirty gallons. (Jn 2:6)

Hail Mary

Jesus told them, "Fill the jars with water." So they filled them to the brim. (Jn 2:7)

Hail Mary

Then he told them, "Draw some out now and take it to the headwaiter." So they took it. (Jn 2:8)

Hail Mary

And when the headwaiter tasted the water that had become wine, without knowing where it came from, . . . the headwaiter called the bridegroom. (Jn 2:9)

Hail Mary

The headwaiter called the bridegroom and said to him, "Everyone serves good wine first, and then when people have drunk freely, an inferior one; but you have kept the good wine until now." (Jn 2:9–10)

Hail Mary

Jesus did this as the beginning of his signs in Cana in Galilee and so revealed his glory, and his disciples began to believe in him. (Jn 2:11)

Hail Mary

Glory Be

Fatima Prayer

Third
Luminous Mystery
The Proclamation of the Kingdom

Our Father

> From that time on, Jesus began to preach and say, "Repent, for the kingdom of heaven is at hand." (Mt 4:17)

Hail Mary

> He went around all of Galilee, teaching in their synagogues, proclaiming the gospel of the kingdom, and curing every disease and illness among the people. (Mt 4:23)

Hail Mary

> "To you who hear I say, love your enemies, do good to those who hate you, bless those who curse you, pray for those who mistreat you." (Lk 6:27–28)

Hail Mary

"Do to others as you would have them do to you. For if you love those who love you, what credit is that to you? Even sinners love those who love them. And if you do good to those who do good to you, what credit is that to you? Even sinners do the same." (Lk 6:31–33)

Hail Mary

"Not everyone who says to me, 'Lord, Lord,' will enter the kingdom of heaven, but only the one who does the will of my Father in heaven." (Mt 7:21)

Hail Mary

"Amen, I say to you, whoever does not accept the kingdom of God like a child will not enter it." (Lk 18:17)

Hail Mary

"It is easier for a camel to pass through the eye of a needle than for one who is rich to enter the kingdom of God." (Mt 19:24)

Hail Mary

Luminous Mysteries

When the disciples heard this, they were greatly astonished and said, "Who then can be saved?" (Mt 19:25)

Hail Mary

Jesus looked at them and said, "For human beings this is impossible, but for God all things are possible." (Mt 19:26)

Hail Mary

He summoned the crowd with his disciples and said to them, "Whoever wishes to come after me must deny himself, take up his cross, and follow me." (Mk 8:34)

Hail Mary

Glory Be

Fatima Prayer

Fourth Luminous Mystery
The Transfiguration

Our Father

> Jesus took Peter, James, and John his brother, and led them up a high mountain by themselves. (Mt 17:1)

Hail Mary

> And he was transfigured before them, and his clothes became dazzling white, such as no fuller on earth could bleach them. (Mk 9:2–3)

Hail Mary

> And behold, two men were conversing with him, Moses and Elijah, who appeared in glory and spoke of his exodus that he was going to accomplish in Jerusalem. (Lk 9:30–31)

Hail Mary

> Peter said to Jesus in reply, "Rabbi, it is good that we are here!" (Mk 9:5)

Hail Mary

> "Let us make three tents: one for you, one for Moses, and one for Elijah." He hardly knew what to say, they were so terrified. (Mk 9:5–6)

Hail Mary

> While he was still speaking, behold, a bright cloud cast a shadow over them. (Mt 17:5)

Hail Mary

> Then from the cloud came a voice that said, "This is my chosen Son; listen to him." (Lk 9:35)

Hail Mary

> Jesus came and touched them, saying, "Rise, and do not be afraid." (Mt 17:7)

Hail Mary

Suddenly, looking around, they no longer saw anyone but Jesus alone with them. (Mk 9:8)

Hail Mary

As they were coming down from the mountain, he charged them not to relate what they had seen to anyone, except when the Son of Man had risen from the dead. (Mk 9:9)

Hail Mary

Glory Be

Fatima Prayer

Fifth

Luminous Mystery

The Institution
of the Eucharist

Our Father

> "I am the bread of life. Your ancestors ate
> the manna in the desert, but they died; this
> is the bread that comes down from heaven
> so that one may eat it and not die." (Jn
> 6:48–50)

Hail Mary

> "I am the living bread that came down
> from heaven; whoever eats this bread will
> live forever; and the bread that I will give is
> my flesh for the life of the world." (Jn 6:51)

Hail Mary

> Now the Passover of the Jews was near,
> and many went up from the country
> to Jerusalem before Passover to purify

themselves. They looked for Jesus and said to one another as they were in the temple area, "What do you think? That he will not come to the feast?" (Jn 11:55–56)

Hail Mary

On the first day of the Feast of Unleavened Bread, the disciples approached Jesus and said, "Where do you want us to prepare for you to eat the Passover?" (Mt 26:17)

Hail Mary

He said, "Go into the city to a certain man and tell him, 'The teacher says, "My appointed time draws near; in your house I shall celebrate the Passover with my disciples."'" (Mt 26:18)

Hail Mary

The disciples then did as Jesus had ordered, and prepared the Passover. (Mt 26:19)

Hail Mary

When it was evening, he came with the Twelve. . . . While they were eating, he took bread, said the blessing, broke it, and gave it to them, and said, "Take it; this is my body." (Mk 14:17, 22)

Hail Mary

Then he took a cup, gave thanks, and gave it to them, and they all drank from it. He said to them, "This is my blood of the covenant, which will be shed for many." (Mk 14:23–24)

Hail Mary

"I tell you, from now on I shall not drink this fruit of the vine until the day when I drink it with you new in the kingdom of my Father." (Mt 26:29)

Hail Mary

Then, after singing a hymn, they went out to the Mount of Olives. (Mt 26:30)

Hail Mary

Glory Be

Fatima Prayer

Salve Regina

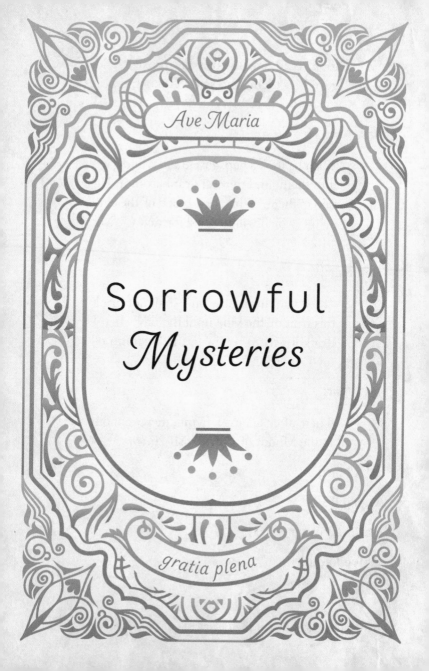

Ave Maria

Sorrowful *Mysteries*

gratia plena

O Jesus, be mindful of your own
bitter Passion and do not permit the
loss of souls redeemed at so dear a
price of your most precious Blood. O
Jesus, when I consider the great price
of your Blood, I rejoice at its immen-
sity, for one drop alone would have
been enough for the salvation of all
sinners.

—St. Faustina Kowalksa

First

Sorrowful Mystery

The Agony in the Garden

Our Father

> Jesus came with them to a place called Gethsemane, and he said to his disciples, "Sit here while I go over there to pray." (Mt 26:36)

Hail Mary

> When he arrived at the place he said to them, "Pray that you may not undergo the test." (Lk 22:40)

Hail Mary

> He advanced a little and fell prostrate in prayer, saying, "My Father, if it is possible, let this cup pass from me; yet, not as I will, but as you will." (Mt 26:39)

Hail Mary

> And to strengthen him an angel from heaven appeared to him. He was in such agony and he prayed so fervently that his sweat became like drops of blood falling on the ground. (Lk 22:43–44)

Hail Mary

> When he returned to his disciples he found them asleep. He said to Peter, "So you could not keep watch with me for one hour?" (Mt 26:40)

Hail Mary

> "Watch and pray that you may not undergo the test. The spirit is willing but the flesh is weak." (Mk 14:38)

Hail Mary

> Then he returned once more and found them asleep, for they could not keep their eyes open. He left them and withdrew again and prayed a third time, saying the same thing again. (Mt 26:43–44)

Hail Mary

Sorrowful Mysteries

Then he returned to his disciples and said to them, "Are you still sleeping and taking your rest? Behold, the hour is at hand when the Son of Man is to be handed over to sinners." (Mt 26:45)

Hail Mary

"Get up, let us go. See, my betrayer is at hand." (Mk 14:42)

Hail Mary

Judas his betrayer also knew the place, because Jesus had often met there with his disciples. So Judas got a band of soldiers and guards from the chief priests and the Pharisees and went there with lanterns, torches, and weapons. (Jn 18:2–3)

Hail Mary

Glory Be

Fatima Prayer

Second
Sorrowful Mystery

The Scourging
at the Pillar

Our Father

> They bound Jesus, led him away, and
> handed him over to Pilate. Pilate ques-
> tioned him, "Are you the king of the
> Jews?" (Mk 15:1–2)

Hail Mary

> Jesus answered, "My kingdom does not
> belong to this world." (Jn 18:36)

Hail Mary

> "For this I was born and for this I came
> into the world, to testify to the truth." (Jn
> 18:37)

Hail Mary

[Pilate] went out to the Jews and said to them, "I find no guilt in him. Therefore I shall have him flogged and then release him." (Jn 18:38; Lk 23:16)

Hail Mary

Then Pilate took Jesus and had him scourged. (Jn 19:1)

Hail Mary

Seized and condemned, he was taken away. Who would have thought any more of his destiny? (Is 53:8)

Hail Mary

Though harshly treated, he submitted and did not open his mouth; Like a lamb led to slaughter or a sheep silent before shearers, he did not open his mouth. (Is 53:7)

Hail Mary

He was pierced for our sins, crushed for our iniquity. (Is 53:5)

Hail Mary

It was our pain that he bore, our sufferings he endured. (Is 53:4)

Hail Mary

He bore the punishment that makes us whole, by his wounds we were healed. (Is 53:5)

Hail Mary

Glory Be

Fatima Prayer

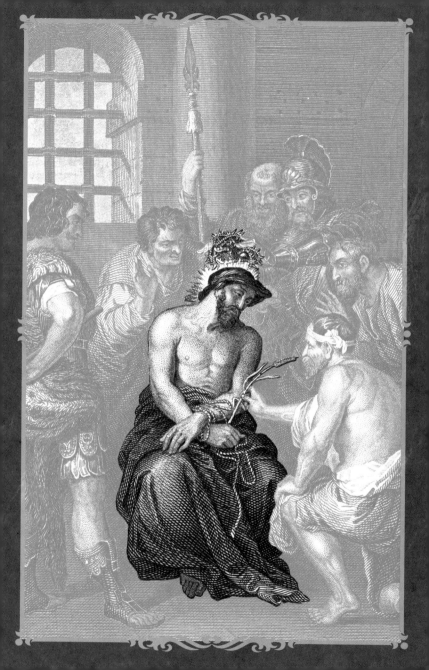

Third
Sorrowful Mystery
The Crowning with Thorns

Our Father

> The soldiers led him away inside the palace, that is, the praetorium, and assembled the whole cohort. They stripped off his clothes and threw a military cloak about him. (Mk 15:16; Mt 27:28)

Hail Mary

> Weaving a crown out of thorns, they placed it on his head, and a reed in his right hand. (Mt 27:29)

Hail Mary

> And kneeling before him, they mocked him, saying, "Hail, King of the Jews!" (Mt 27:29)

Hail Mary

> They spat upon him and took the reed and kept striking him on the head. (Mt 27:30)

Hail Mary

> [Pilate] went out to the Jews and said to them, "I find no guilt in him." He took water and washed his hands in the sight of the crowd, saying, "I am innocent of this man's blood. Look to it yourselves." (Jn 18:38; Mt 27:24)

Hail Mary

> So Jesus came out, wearing the crown of thorns and the purple cloak. (Jn 19:5)

Hail Mary

> [Pilate] said to the Jews, "Behold, your king!" They cried out, "Take him away, take him away! Crucify him!" (Jn 19:14–15)

Hail Mary

Sorrowful Mysteries

Pilate said to them, "Why? What evil has he done?" They only shouted the louder, "Crucify him." (Mk 15:14)

Hail Mary

Pilate said to them, "Shall I crucify your king?" The chief priests answered, "We have no king but Caesar." (Jn 19:15)

Hail Mary

So Pilate, wishing to satisfy the crowd, . . . handed him over to be crucified. (Mk 15:15)

Hail Mary

Glory Be

Fatima Prayer

Third: The Crowning with Thorns

Fourth
Sorrowful Mystery
The Carrying of the Cross

Our Father

> [Jesus] said to all, "If anyone wishes to come after me, he must deny himself and take up his cross daily and follow me." (Lk 9:23)

Hail Mary

> "For whoever wishes to save his life will lose it, but whoever loses his life for my sake and that of the gospel will save it." (Mk 8:35)

Hail Mary

> And carrying the cross himself he went out to what is called the Place of the Skull, in Hebrew, Golgotha. (Jn 19:17)

Hail Mary

> As they led him away they took hold of a certain Simon, a Cyrenian, who was coming in from the country; and after laying the cross on him, they made him carry it behind Jesus. (Lk 23:26)

Hail Mary

> "Take my yoke upon you and learn from me." (Mt 11:29)

Hail Mary

> "For I am meek and humble of heart." (Mt 11:29)

Hail Mary

> "And you will find rest for yourselves. For my yoke is easy, and my burden light." (Mt 11:29–30)

Hail Mary

> A large crowd of people followed Jesus, including many women who mourned and lamented him. (Lk 23:27)

Hail Mary

Jesus turned to them and said, "Daughters of Jerusalem, do not weep for me; weep instead for yourselves and for your children." (Lk 23:28)

Hail Mary

"For if these things are done when the wood is green what will happen when it is dry?" (Lk 23:31)

Hail Mary

Glory Be

Fatima Prayer

Fifth

Sorrowful Mystery

The Crucifixion

Our Father

> When they came to the place called the Skull, they crucified him. (Lk 23:33)

Hail Mary

> Jesus said, "Father, forgive them, they know not what they do." (Lk 23:34)

Hail Mary

> Now one of the criminals hanging there reviled Jesus, saying, "Are you not the Messiah? Save yourself and us." The other, however, rebuking him, said in reply, "Have you no fear of God?" (Lk 23:39–40)

Hail Mary

> Then he said, "Jesus, remember me when you come into your kingdom." [Jesus]

replied to him, "Amen, I say to you, today you will be with me in Paradise." (Lk 23:42–43)

Hail Mary

Standing by the cross of Jesus were his mother . . . and the disciple . . . whom he loved. (Jn 19:25–26)

Hail Mary

He said to his mother, "Woman, behold, your son." Then he said to the disciple, "Behold, your mother." And from that hour the disciple took her into his home. (Jn 19:26–27)

Hail Mary

It was now about noon and darkness came over the whole land until three in the afternoon because of an eclipse of the sun. (Lk 23:44–45)

Hail Mary

Then the veil of the temple was torn down the middle. (Lk 23:45)

Hail Mary

> Jesus cried out in a loud voice, "Father, into your hands I commend my spirit." (Lk 23:46)

Hail Mary

> When he had said this he breathed his last. (Lk 23:46)

Hail Mary

Glory Be

Fatima Prayer

Salve Regina

Fifth: The Crucifixion

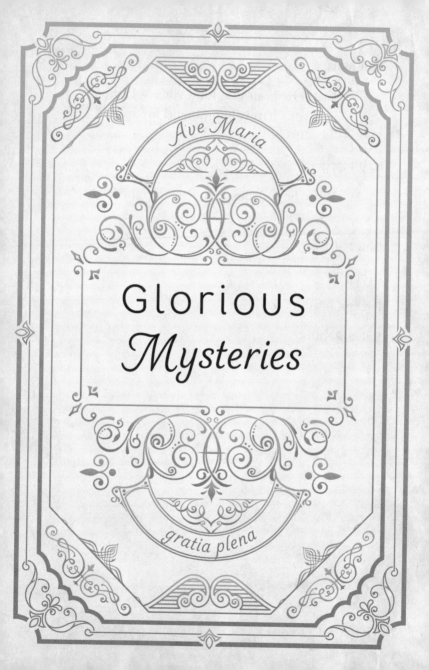

Ave Maria

Glorious
Mysteries

gratia plena

This is the night,
when Christ broke the prison-bars of
    death
and rose victorious from the
    underworld.
Our birth would have been no gain,
had we not been redeemed.
O wonder of your humble care for us!
O love, O charity beyond all telling,
to ransom a slave you gave away
    your Son!
O truly necessary sin of Adam,
destroyed completely by the Death
    of Christ!
O happy fault
that earned so great, so glorious a
    Redeemer!
                  —From the Exsultet

First
Glorious Mystery
The Resurrection

Our Father

> "Amen, amen, I say to you, you will weep and mourn, while the world rejoices; you will grieve, but your grief will become joy." (Jn 16:20)

Hail Mary

> "You also are now in anguish. But I will see you again, and your hearts will rejoice, and no one will take your joy away from you." (Jn 16:22)

Hail Mary

> At daybreak on the first day of the week they took the spices they had prepared and went to the tomb. (Lk 24:1)

Hail Mary

> An angel of the Lord descended from heaven, approached, rolled back the stone, and sat upon it. His appearance was like lightning and his clothing was white as snow. (Mt 28:2–3)

Hail Mary

> The angel said to the women . . . "Do not be afraid! I know that you are seeking Jesus the crucified. He is not here." (Mt 28:5–6)

Hail Mary

> "He has been raised just as he said. Come and see the place where he lay." (Mt 28:6)

Hail Mary

> "Then go quickly and tell his disciples, 'He has been raised from the dead, and he is going before you to Galilee; there you will see him.'" (Mt 28:7)

Hail Mary

Glorious Mysteries

Then they went away quickly from the tomb, fearful yet overjoyed, and ran to announce this to his disciples. (Mt 28:8)

Hail Mary

"I am the resurrection and the life; whoever believes in me, even if he dies, will live." (Jn 11:25)

Hail Mary

"And everyone who lives and believes in me will never die." (Jn 11:26)

Hail Mary

Glory Be

Fatima Prayer

First: The Resurrection

Second

Glorious Mystery

The Ascension

Our Father

> Then he led them [out] as far as Bethany, raised his hands, and blessed them. (Lk 24:50; brackets in the original)

Hail Mary

> Jesus approached and said to them, "All power in heaven and on earth has been given to me." (Mt 28:18)

Hail Mary

> "Go, therefore, and make disciples of all nations." (Mt 28:19)

Hail Mary

> "Baptiz[e] them in the name of the Father, and of the Son, and of the holy Spirit. (Mt 28:19)

Hail Mary

> "[Teach] them to observe all that I have commanded you." (Mt 28:20)

Hail Mary

> "And behold, I am with you always, until the end of the age." (Mt 28:20)

Hail Mary

> When he said this, as they were looking on, he was lifted up, and a cloud took him from their sight. (Acts 1:9)

Hail Mary

> The Lord Jesus, after he spoke to them, was taken up to heaven and took his seat at the right hand of God. (Mk 16:19)

Hail Mary

> While they were looking intently at the sky as he was going, suddenly two men dressed in white garments stood beside them. (Acts 1:10)

Hail Mary

They said, "Men of Galilee, why are you standing there looking at the sky? This Jesus who has been taken up from you into heaven will return in the same way as you have seen him going to heaven." (Acts 1:11)

Hail Mary

Glory Be

Fatima Prayer

Third

Glorious Mystery

The Descent of the Holy Spirit

Our Father

> When the time for Pentecost was fulfilled, they were all in one place together. (Acts 2:1)

Hail Mary

> And suddenly there came from the sky a noise like a strong driving wind, and it filled the entire house in which they were. (Acts 2:2)

Hail Mary

> Then there appeared to them tongues as of fire, which parted and came to rest on each one of them. (Acts 2:3)

Hail Mary

> And they were all filled with the holy Spirit and began to speak in different tongues, as the Spirit enabled them to proclaim. (Acts 2:4)

Hail Mary

> Now there were devout Jews from every nation under heaven staying in Jerusalem. (Acts 2:5)

Hail Mary

> At this sound, they gathered in a large crowd, but they were confused because each one heard them speaking in his own language. (Acts 2:6)

Hail Mary

> They were astounded, and in amazement they asked, "Are not all these people who are speaking Galileans?" (Acts 2:7)

Hail Mary

> "Then how does each of us hear them in his own native language?" (Acts 2:8)

Glorious Mysteries

> [Peter said,] "This is what was spoken through the prophet Joel: 'It will come to pass in the last days,' God says, 'that I will pour out a portion of my spirit upon all flesh. Your sons and daughters shall prophesy, your young men shall see visions, your old men shall dream dreams.'" (Acts 2:16–17)

Hail Mary

> "'And I will work wonders in the heavens above and signs on the earth below; blood, fire, and a cloud of smoke.'" (Acts 2:19)

Hail Mary

Glory Be

Fatima Prayer

Fourth

Glorious Mystery

The Assumption of Mary

Our Father

> "Arise, my friend, my beautiful one, and come!" (Sg 2:10)

Hail Mary

> "For see, the winter is past, the rains are over and gone." (Sg 2:11)

Hail Mary

> "Let me see your face, let me hear your voice, For your voice is sweet, and your face is lovely." (Sg 2:14)

Hail Mary

> Then God's temple in heaven was opened, and the ark of his covenant could be seen in the temple. There were flashes of

lightning, rumblings, and peals of thunder, an earthquake, and a violent hailstorm. (Rv 11:19)

Hail Mary

A great sign appeared in the sky, a woman clothed with the sun. (Rv 12:1)

Hail Mary

The moon [was] under her feet, and on her head a crown of twelve stars. (Rv 12:1)

Hail Mary

All glorious is the king's daughter as she enters, her raiment threaded with gold; In embroidered apparel she is led to the king. (Ps 45:14–15)

Hail Mary

The maids of her train are presented to the king. They are led in with glad and joyous acclaim; they enter the palace of the king. (Ps 45:16)

Hail Mary

I will make your name renowned through all generations; thus nations shall praise you forever. (Ps 45:18)

Hail Mary

"May the LORD reward what you have done! May you receive a full reward from the LORD, the God of Israel, under whose wings you have come for refuge." (Ru 2:12)

Hail Mary

Glory Be

Fatima Prayer

Fifth

Glorious Mystery

The Coronation of Mary, Queen of Heaven and Earth

Our Father

> Of all the virgins she won his favor and good will. So he placed the royal crown on her head and made her queen. (Est 2:17)

Hail Mary

> I belong to my lover, and my lover belongs to me; he feeds among the lilies. (Sg 6:3)

Hail Mary

> Praise the LORD, for he is good; for his mercy endures forever. (Ps 136:1)

Hail Mary

The king has brought me to his bed chambers. Let us exult and rejoice in you; let us celebrate your love. (Sg 1:4)

Hail Mary

Like a lily among thorns, so is my friend among women. (Sg 2:2)

Hail Mary

How beautiful you are, my friend, how beautiful you are! (Sg 4:1)

Hail Mary

Now, children, listen to me; . . . Listen to instruction and grow wise. (Prv 8:32)

Hail Mary

Happy the one who listens to me, attending daily at my gates, keeping watch at my doorposts. (Prv 8:34)

Hail Mary

For whoever finds me finds life, and wins favor from the LORD. (Prv 8:35)

Hail Mary

Let me dwell in your tent forever, take refuge in the shelter of your wings. (Ps 61:5)

Hail Mary

Glory Be

Fatima Prayer

Appendix

Marian Prayers

The Memorare

> Remember, O most gracious Virgin
>   Mary,
> that never was it known
> that anyone who fled to thy protection,
> implored thy help, or sought thy
>   intercession
> was left unaided.
> Inspired by this confidence,
> I fly unto thee, O Virgin of virgins, my
>   Mother;
> to thee do I come,

before thee I stand, sinful and
    sorrowful.
O Mother of the Word Incarnate,
despise not my petitions,
but in thy mercy, hear and answer me.
Amen.

The Angelus (prayed three times daily)

V. The Angel of the Lord declared
   unto Mary.
R. And she conceived of the Holy
   Spirit.

Hail Mary

V. Behold the handmaid of the Lord.
R. Be it done unto me according to thy
   word.

Hail Mary

V. And the Word was made flesh.
R. And dwelt among us.

Hail Mary

V. Pray for us, O holy Mother of God.
R. That we may be made worthy of
   the promises of Christ.

Let us pray:
Pour forth, we beseech thee, O Lord,
thy grace into our hearts; that we,
to whom the Incarnation of Christ, thy
   Son,

was made known by the message of an
    angel,
may by his Passion and Cross
be brought to the glory of his
    Resurrection.
Through the same Christ Our Lord.
Amen.

Regina Coeli (replaces the Angelus during Lent)

Queen of heaven, rejoice, alleluia.
The Son whom you merited to bear,
    alleluia,
has risen as he said, alleluia.
Rejoice and be glad, O Virgin Mary,
    alleluia!
For the Lord has truly risen, alleluia.

Let us pray:
O God, who through the Resurrection
of your Son, our Lord Jesus Christ,
did vouchsafe to give joy to the world;
grant, we beseech you, that through
his Mother, the Virgin Mary, we may
obtain the joys of everlasting life.
Through the same Christ our Lord.
Amen.

The Magnificat

My soul proclaims the greatness of the
Lord;

my spirit rejoices in God my Savior

for he has looked with favor on his
lowly servant.

From this day all generations will call
me blessed:

the Almighty has done great things for
me,

and holy is his name.

He has mercy on those who fear him

in every generation.

He has shown the strength of his arm;

he has scattered the proud in their
conceit.

He has cast down the mighty from
their thrones

and has lifted up the lowly.

He has filled the hungry with good
things,

and the rich he has sent away empty.

He has come to the help of his servant
Israel

for he remembered his promise of
    mercy,
the promise he made to our fathers,
to Abraham and his children forever.
Amen.

Marian Litany

Litany to the Blessed Virgin Mary (Litany of Loreto)

Lord, have mercy on us.
Christ, have mercy on us.
Lord, have mercy.
Christ, hear us.
Christ, graciously hear us.

God the Father of heaven, *have mercy on us*.
God the Son, Redeemer of the world, *have mercy on us*.
God the Holy Spirit, *have mercy on us*.
Holy Trinity, One God, *have mercy on us*.

Holy Mary, *pray for us*.

Holy Mother of God, *pray for us.*
Holy Virgin of Virgins, *pray for us.*

Mother of Christ, *pray for us.*
Mother of the Church, *pray for us*
Mother of Divine Grace, *pray for us.*
Mother most pure, *pray for us.*
Mother most chaste, *pray for us.*
Mother inviolate, *pray for us.*
Mother most amiable, *pray for us.*
Mother most admirable, *pray for us.*
Mother of Good Counsel, *pray for us.*
Mother of our Creator, *pray for us.*
Mother of our Savior, *pray for us.*

Virgin most prudent, *pray for us.*
Virgin most venerable, *pray for us.*
Virgin most renowned, *pray for us.*
Virgin most powerful, *pray for us.*
Virgin most merciful, *pray for us.*
Virgin most faithful, *pray for us.*

Mirror of justice, *pray for us.*
Seat of wisdom, *pray for us.*
Cause of our joy, *pray for us.*

Spiritual vessel, *pray for us.*
Vessel of honor, *pray for us.*
Singular vessel of devotion, *pray for us.*
Mystical Rose, *pray for us.*
Tower of David, *pray for us.*
Tower of ivory, *pray for us.*
House of gold, *pray for us.*
Ark of the Covenant, *pray for us.*
Gate of heaven, *pray for us.*
Morning star, *pray for us.*
Health of the sick, *pray for us.*
Refuge of sinners, *pray for us.*
Comforter of the afflicted, *pray for us.*
Help of Christians, *pray for us.*

Queen of Angels, *pray for us.*
Queen of patriarchs, *pray for us.*
Queen of prophets, *pray for us.*
Queen of apostles, *pray for us.*
Queen of martyrs, *pray for us.*
Queen of confessors, *pray for us.*
Queen of virgins, *pray for us.*
Queen of all saints, *pray for us.*
Queen conceived without original sin,
    pray for us.

Queen assumed into heaven, *pray for us*.

Queen of the most Holy Rosary, *pray for us*.

Queen of peace, *pray for us*

Lamb of God, who takes away the sins of the world, *spare us, O Lord*.

Lamb of God, who takes away the sins of the world, *graciously hear us, O Lord*.

Lamb of God, who takes away the sins of the world, *have mercy on us*.

V. Pray for us, O Holy Mother of God,

R. *That we may be made worthy of the promises of Christ*.

Let us pray.

Grant, we beseech thee, O Lord God, that we thy servants may enjoy perpetual health of mind and body, and by the glorious intercession of the Blessed Mary, ever Virgin, be delivered from

present sorrow and enjoy everlasting
happiness. Through Christ Our Lord.
Amen.

Marian Novena

(nine days of prayer for a special intention)

Novena to Our Lady of Perpetual Help

Behold, O Mother of Perpetual Help, at your feet a wretched sinner, who has recourse to thee and trusts in you. O Mother of Mercy, have pity on me; I hear all men and women call you the refuge and hope of sinners: be therefore my refuge and my hope. Help me for the love of Jesus Christ: hold out thy hand to a fallen wretch, who commends myself to you and dedicates myself to be your servant forever. I praise and thank God, who of his great mercy has given me this confidence in thee, a sure pledge of my eternal salvation. Alas, it is only too true that in the past I have fallen miserably, because I did not come to you. I know that with your help I shall conquer; I know that you will help me, if I commend myself to you; but I am fearful lest in the occasions of sin I shall forget to call upon you and so I shall be lost. This grace, then, do I ask of you; for this I implore you, as much as I can and know how to do: namely, that in the assaults of hell I may ever run to your protection and may say to you: Mary, help me; Mother of Perpetual Help, permit me not to lose my God.

Hail Mary (three times)

O Mother of Perpetual Help, grant me ever to be able to call upon your powerful name, since your name is the help of the living and the salvation of the dying. Ah, Mary most pure, Mary most sweet, grant that your name from this day forth may be to me the very breath of life. Dear Lady, delay not to come to my assistance whenever I call upon you; for in all the temptations that assail me, in all the necessities that befall me, I will never leave off calling upon you, ever repeating: Mary, Mary. What comfort, what sweetness, what confidence, what tenderness fills my soul at the sound of your name, at the very thought of you! I give thanks to our Lord, who for my sake has given thee a name so sweet, so lovable, so mighty. But I am not content merely to speak thy name; I would utter it for very love of thee; it is my desire that love should ever remind me to name thee, Mother of Perpetual Help.

Hail Mary (three times)

O Mother of Perpetual Help, you art the dispenser of every grace that God grants us in our misery; it is for this cause that he hath made you so powerful, so rich, so kind, that thou mightest assist us in our miseries. Thou art the advocate of the most wretched and abandoned sinners, if they but come unto thee; come once more to my assistance, for I commend myself to you. In thy hands I place my eternal salvation;

to you I entrust my soul. Enroll me among your most faithful servants; take me under thy protection and it is enough for me: yes, for if thou protect me, I shall fear nothing; not my sins, for you wilt obtain for me their pardon and remission; not the evil spirits, for thou art mightier than all the powers of hell; not even Jesus, my Judge, for he is appeased by a single prayer from you. I fear only that through my own negligence I may forget to recommend myself to thee and so I shall be lost. My dear Lady, obtain for me the forgiveness of my sins, love for Jesus, final perseverance, and the grace to have recourse to you at all times, O Mother of Perpetual Help.
Amen.

Hail Mary (three times)

Appendix

Marian Consecration

Act of Consecration to Mary
(written by St. Maximilian Kolbe)

O Immaculata, Queen of heaven and earth, refuge of sinners and our most loving Mother, God has willed to entrust the entire order of mercy to you. I, (name), a repentant sinner, cast myself at your feet humbly imploring you to take me, with all that I am and have, wholly to yourself as your possession and property. Please make of me, of all my powers of soul and body, of my whole life, death, and eternity, whatever most pleases you.

If it pleases you, use all that I am and have without reserve, wholly to accomplish what was said of you: "She will crush your head," and, "You alone have destroyed all heresies in the world." Let me be a fit instrument in your immaculate and merciful hands for introducing and increasing your glory to the maximum in all the many strayed and indifferent souls, and thus help extend as far as possible the blessed kingdom of the most Sacred Heart of Jesus. For wherever you enter, you obtain the grace of conversion and growth in holiness, since it is through your hands that all graces come to us from the most Sacred Heart of Jesus.

V. Allow me to praise you, O sacred Virgin.

R. Give me strength against your enemies.

ALSO AVAILABLE

The Ave Guide to Eucharistic Adoration

Spending time in adoration of the Blessed Sacrament
is an important Catholic practice that honors
the Real Presence of Christ in the Eucharist.
The Ave Guide to Eucharistic Adoration offers a rich array
of prayers, devotions, meditations, and Church teachings
to read during your quiet time with the Lord,
whether you have fifteen minutes or an entire holy hour.
Elegant, vintage lithographs and engravings taken from
traditional prayer books, psalters, and Bibles
accompany each of the four parts of the book,
which are organized around the four parts of the Mass:

 · Penance   · Scripture

✝ · Sacrifice   🤝 · Service

In addition to traditional prayers and devotions, the reflection
material includes profiles and writings of saints, encyclicals,
writings of the church fathers, short Bible passages from
the *New American Bible* (the translation used in the Mass),
and explanations of Church teachings. Each reading is
accompanied by questions for reflection and is designed for
fifteen minutes of personal time before the Blessed Sacrament.